THE
LADDER
OF
SUCCESS

A Journey for all

By Gloria M. Cox

I would like to thank
God for loving me, Pastor Steve and Sister Kathy
for teaching me, and all my family for their
support and help

TABLE OF CONTENTS

FORWARD

Changing lives is what Jesus is all about. What you are about to read is the true story of one such person. Her life changed, her marriage rearranged, and her family was reunited by the wonderful truths she found in the love of God. You are about to see that knowing the truth is not all there is to Christianity. When you truly have a revelation of "His" love; it takes all you know and brings to you an understanding of that knowledge in application to you.

A changed life is the result of an inward change. When you change the root, you get different fruit. Many today are wanting and desiring something different in their lives and marriages, and are willing to do just about anything to get those changes. Will we do the one thing that could change everything? That "one thing" is to change our thinking, the basics comprises our entire life. As Gloria shares these truths with you and the practical application of the Word of God, please understand that this is not a book that gives you the answers to change your facts and circumstance or solve all your problems. The principles shared in this book will help you to change you, and will help you to continue to live that changed life. It will enable you to maintain the change and help you learn to live in daily victory while dealing with the "stuff" that life is

4

full of. We often think that, "if this was different" or "when that changes" or "if that person would treat me different", things would be better. When we realize those things won't give us victory, we see why we continue to struggle with the same problems.

There is not a greater blessing than to see people in your local church becoming winners in life and agents of change, influencing the lives of others and bringing them into the Kingdom of God. This is what Jesus is all about, changing lives and becoming salt and light to others. This book is a little salt and pepper to season your life. It's truth that will set you free and help you to be all you were created to be in Him. The greatest thing that you can ever find is who you are in Him, so you can say, "I am free to be me." God is not looking for people that are humanly faultless. He is looking for those that will not be ashamed to let another see them in their human frailty; others truly need to be able to see God's grace at work. Get ready to enjoy the rest of your life. God has already made the appropriate provisions and is waiting on you to receive His love.
Blessings to you!

Pastor Steve Cox, (no relation)
Resurrection Life Church
Moss Bluff, LA
December 2002

WARNING

I suggest very strongly, if you are not

ready for the Lord to change you,

DO NOT READ THIS BOOK

INTRODUCTION

As a new Christian, God gave me what I am about to share with you. Over the last 21+ years, He has expanded it and gave me the opportunity to apply all these truths. Did I always get it right the first time? No, but He didn't expect me too! He doesn't expect you to either. All He asks is we try and keep trying. My hope is that you are able to take at least one thing to heart out of these pages.

1. BEFORE THE BEGINNING

Before the beginning, I found myself in a very bad place. My situation didn't happen over night, it had taken about seven years of slow erosion to reach bottom. I had finally lost all hope, so one night in September with nowhere to go or the ability to get there, I said one simple prayer. "Lord, I don't know what to do, help me!" Waking the next morning, I felt a peace over me. The depression had lifted, and I was left with a sense of energy and purpose; although I didn't know what that purpose was. As the day progressed, doors began to open and as I stepped through each one, my peace increased. I knew that I was doing the right thing.

Not long after, I started going to a counseling group that focused on supporting each other and emphasized the concept of looking for our 'higher power'. I knew in my mind that God was my higher power, and I knew He had answered my prayer but that was all I knew. I believed in God, but I didn't believe in the concept of church. I had gone to church off and on all my life and had been turned away by the hypocrisy I experienced. I didn't feel I needed to go to church to have people look down their noses at me. I had tried reading the Bible several times throughout my life but always wound up arguing with it, putting it down not to be picked up for years. I had even been baptized twice. After a few weeks, someone very close to me expressed concern over my salvation and invited me to go to church. I had reservations but it was important to him, so what did I have to lose in going.

During the service, the pastor had an alter call. I had an inner drive to go but my feet and a fear of the unknown kept me from moving. The pastor must have been reading my mind because he directed the congregation to reach out to the people around them and offer their help to come forward. When the lady in front of me turned and offered her hand, I could say nothing. I started crying as I took her hand. She went forward with me, and I accepted Jesus into my heart. I had never experienced anything like that before, the feelings were overpowering. I could not understand why I was crying because I felt happy, almost euphoric. Life hasn't been the same since that day and is only getting better. They gave me a little book that walked me through the book of John, and I understood what John was saying. God was talking to me through His written word. A desire was sparked in me to not only learn more but also to apply what I was learning to everyday life. I understood that what I had experienced in the past was religious thinking. What I am experiencing now is Christianity.

The church that I accepted Jesus in was not teaching what I needed to learn at that time, so I tried a new one. As soon as I walked through the front doors, I felt at home. The message that was being taught was exactly what I needed to hear. It was based on the practical application of God's word. It was a strange experience to be happy and crying at the same time, but it became a regular occurrence during praise and worship. There were a lot of things happening to and around me that I didn't understand but my desire to learn was great. I was reading the Bible and any other material I could find, and I was growing in understanding. The more I learned, the more I wanted to learn, experience, and apply to my life. I realized that being a Christian wasn't just knowing what the Bible said or avoiding things that would send me to hell, but rather a relationship. I also realized the type of relationship I have with God is up to me and does not depend on anyone else.

My husband was away one night so I was cleaning the house and doing laundry when I heard the Lord tell me to write my testimony. It was as loud as someone standing right next to me. Never experiencing the voice of God before, my reaction was "Ya, right, I'm going nuts!" As I went on about my business, I heard it again, only this time He was reminding me of things I had experienced, so I knew I had to write them down. When I would think I was done, I would go do something around the house only to be sent back to write more. To my amazement, this went on until 1:30 in the morning. I was able to get all my work done, and the testimony written. Even more amazing was that I woke up at 5:30 A.M. fully rested and ready to go to work.

Keep in mind I had been baptized twice already, but I realized I had done them for the wrong reasons. As I was growing in the Lord, I learned that being baptized was a symbol, 'an outward sign of an inward change'. It was making a statement to the world that God was an active part of my life. I wanted to be baptized the first time because at the age of eight, one of my friends was going to be. The second time was that my girls were being baptized and I couldn't ask them to do something I wasn't willing to do myself. I have always heard 'the third time is the charm'; this time was for the change that had taken place in my heart. The third time also seemed to be a test of faith. Looking back, it was rather comical. God does have a since of humor!

When I got to church the day of my baptism, everyone was concerned about the temperature of the water. It was January and they had emptied the water heater into the baptismal. The church members had even boiled water on the stove to add to it, but the water was ice cold. It was suggested that I test the water and maybe wait for another time, but all I could say was, "I'll be bathed in the warmth of the Lord!" Those were the only words that would come to my mind or out of my mouth. I never tested the water. I am very sensitive to being cold, I don't like it at all, but when I got in the water, I wasn't cold. About the time I completely sat down, one of the ladies in the congregation got up to give a short testimony. When she was done, my sister-in-law got up to give the congregation a testimony about me. She told them some of what had brought me to where I was. It was very touching but keep in mind; I'm still sitting in ice water. My teeth were chattering but I still didn't feel cold. I was truly bathed in the warmth of the Lord, and I never doubted that I would be. I think He was making a point about trusting Him. At one point, I told the pastor who was standing next to the baptismal, 'even John the Baptist got in the water.' I don't know what the actual temperature of the water was, but my skin hurt for three days after if that gives you any idea.

God has the great ability to change our plans and he did mine. It was Friday and my weekend plans were to get my house cleaned, laundry done, go to a baby shower, go to church, and take my girls to a "Youth on Fire" meeting but that isn't what happened. Saturday morning came and I was on my way to Shreveport, LA with my father-in-law to pick up my husband's uncle and his truck from the hospital. It is about a 5-hour trip from where we lived. Looking back, it was God's way of giving me time just to be in His presence. Most people have the radio on but ours was broken and my father-in-law was hard of hearing. During the trip up, God gave me an illustration of a ladder. The illustration grew little by little, until it was a full concept. When we got to the hotel, I just wanted to take a bath and relax, but God wanted me to write the illustration down. I got out of the tub, dried off, got dressed, and with wet hair walked to the store for a pad of paper. Once written, I called my sister-in-law to share it. As I was reading, she was listening and waiting for what it had to do with me, but it never came. When I was finished, she told me it sounded like I was writing a book. Since then, this image has grown into what you are about to read.

I had put up an argument that night in the hotel about writing anything, but as you can see, God knows best. It doesn't matter that I can't spell or that I hadn't been a Christian very long. What does matter is that I am obedient to what God wants. You will be blessed by the knowledge God has given me.

2. TO BELIEVE OR NOT TO BELIEVE

Have you sat down and thought about how you got where you are and where are you going from here? This question applies to our walk in the natural and spiritual life. Have you thought of your spiritual life's journey being your 'Ladder of Success'? Well, it is and here is how it works! Our spiritual ladder starts when we answer one question within ourselves, to believe[1] or not to believe? There is no gray area here; we either do or don't believe it.

To help understand how to go from being an unbeliever[2] to a believer, we need to understand what it is to have belief[3] as explained in the footnotes. If we think about that definition a minute, then we can settle[4] an issue for ourselves by researching it to prove whether it's right or wrong. No one can do it for us. We must make our own decision.

---

[1] To believe is to have confidence in the truth or the reliability of something without proof.
[2] Unbeliever is a person that is skeptic, a person who doesn't accept all or some part of something. Unbelief is especially expressed in mater of doctrine or religions faith.
[3] Belief is to trust, to have a conviction that is settled, profound, or earnestly believed is right. To hold a system of principle doctrines as true, or to settle or establish an opinion or principle.
[4] Settle is to appoint, fix, or resolve and conclusively; agree upon, to make stable, place in a fixed position on a permanent basis.

I was an unbeliever! I believed there was a God, but had no use for church, didn't read my Bible, and only prayed when I needed something. I didn't understand anything. As a result, I didn't have faith. I said that one prayer that night out of total desperation; God reached down, picked me up by the collar, and placed me down on His path. He dusted me off, combed my hair, gave me all the tools I needed to decide for myself, and pointed the way to my ladder. It was up to me to take that first step, but He has guided my steps ever since.

I have come to realize the difference between what I had experienced in the past (religious thinking) and what I am now experiencing (Christianity). I was being preached at when I was going to church before. Being told the rules of a religion not how to walk with God. I didn't know how to apply God's word to my everyday life, nor was I seeing it applied in other people. I have found that being able to use God's Word comes from understanding. I was never taught about having a relationship with Him. Now I am learning what He wants for me, how to have a relationship with Him, and I feel His love. I also see God's ways in the people around me. God is real in my life, Jesus is my Savior, and Holy Spirit is my friend. The Bible is not just a book to me anymore. It is the revealed will of God, and Holy Spirit guides me through the pages of the wonderful book. God speaks to me through His written Word. To think of the Bible in worldly terms, it could be called the best self help book ever written.

There are two types of unbelievers. The first doesn't know that something is missing in his/her life and is apparently happy. These people won't change their minds even if a catastrophe happens. The second type doesn't know what is missing but does know there is a void of some kind and is searching to fill it. These unbelievers are like a rough diamond working its way up to the surface to be found, having the rough edges cut off and turned into a beautiful stone. This second type could also be described as a dry sponge lost in the wilderness waiting for something it can soak up until it is overflowing.

During conversations about God, I have invited many unbelievers to join me at church. One excuse I have heard repeatedly is, "If I walk in a church, the roof will fall in." They are under the misconception that they must fix their sins before God will accept them. The truth is, God doesn't care what you have done or even where you are when you come to Him. He knows all that! He just wants you to come. I don't go to church to get God in my life; I go because God is in my life. You don't even have to go to church to receive Jesus in your heart. Christians attend church as a part of their commitment to God. They want to gain more understanding of His Word. Having God in our lives is an everyday thing, not just on Sundays. Sundays are just His special day. When I came to Jesus, it was two weeks before I realized I hadn't said one curse word. It was God that changed me. If you are an unbeliever looking for something: don't stop!

> (NIV Luke 11:9-10, *"So I say to you: Ask and it will be given to you; seek and you will find; knock and the door will be opened to you. For everyone who asks receives; he who seeks finds; and to him who knocks, the door will be opened."*)

Repeat after me: "God, I know that something is missing in my life. I don't have a relationship with your son, Jesus. If He is what I am looking for, help me to develop a relationship with Him." He will answer you! My recommendation is to read the Gospel of John in the New Testament. It is written to the unbeliever and new believer. Settle the matter once and for all and step up to your ladder of success.

3. THE LADDER OF SUCCESS

What is the first thing that comes to mind when you think of your ladder of success? For most people I have talked to, it is defined as the steps one takes to reach the top of their chosen careers. That leaves me with the question of 'what then'? The goal has been reached so what is the next goal or do we just stop? Some people know from an early age what they want to do with their lives, but others wander around from job to job or class to class looking for direction. I went into the Air Force at the age of 18 with the intention of making it my career, but life changed that plan and I became a wanderer. Like everyone, priorities change.

I am a visual person, so God deals with me in illustrations. He described His ladder of success on that trip to Shreveport. It is constructed just like a regular ladder with legs and rungs, but with one distinct difference. It is never ending. The legs represent God's direction, and the rungs represent Jesus working in our lives. God's ladder also comes with two more very special items; a platform exists between segments to allow us a resting place, and a safety line which is Holy Spirit. Holy Spirit will catch us when we falter or fall. I have kept Him on his toes because I have faltered and for sure fallen more than a few times. He has always been there to pick me up.

The first type of unbeliever I described earlier will wander around the ladder and never see it, while the second type knows it's there but doesn't know what it represents. When they figure it out and take that first step, they have accepted Jesus as their Savior and are now baby (new) Christians. I am happy to say that was me!

For me, the first segment went fast. God was filling my sponge as quickly as I could absorb everything coming my way until I was overflowing. The more I soaked up, the more I wanted, and the more I wanted to share. Then came a time when what I was receiving slowed down. I felt like something was wrong. I realized God was giving me the time I needed to get comfortable in my own skin. I had reached my first platform, so it was time to reflect on all I had learned and get ready for the next segment of my ladder.

Okay, I have made it to my first platform. I love the comfort and view from where I am. This can be dangerous! It is at this comfort level that many new Christians will stop growing in the Lord. Some may get discouraged and turn away. This discouragement comes from not understanding that God is about to provide them a situation that will give them opportunity to apply what they have learned. So, they don't look for the next step. We have a choice of wrapping our arms around the legs of the ladder for security and staying in our comfort zone or stepping out. After staying at that level for a while, I started thinking and eventually I asked, "Ok Lord, what next?" At this point we better be prepared because God is about to show us something new.

The rungs can be compared to branches of a grapevine. God uses rungs to cast away dead branches that don't produce fruit. What does that mean for us? God will take us through periods of casting things out of our lives that aren't from Him and don't benefit us in our walk. God doesn't expect us to be perfect; He wants us to try. That's why we have Holy Spirit to help. Why do you think the Bible says, "Do not look to the left or the right, look straight ahead"? As humans, we follow our eyes. If we look left, we go left. If we look right, we go right. Only distractions from what God wants for us are to the left or right. God is telling us to stay focused on him by looking straight ahead.

Each of us has had different experiences throughout our lives. No one is the same. Throughout the Bible, Jesus never healed anyone the same way. How He healed me through my ladder will be different from how He heals you through yours. Just know, He will heal you!

The most important thing about the progression up my ladder I found was it requires a relationship with Him. We must allow ourselves to communicate with Him. It's up to us how much or how little that communication is. I had a lot to learn in the relationship area and once again, He used an illustration.

4. RELATIONSHIPS

Dartboard Illustration of Basic Relationships

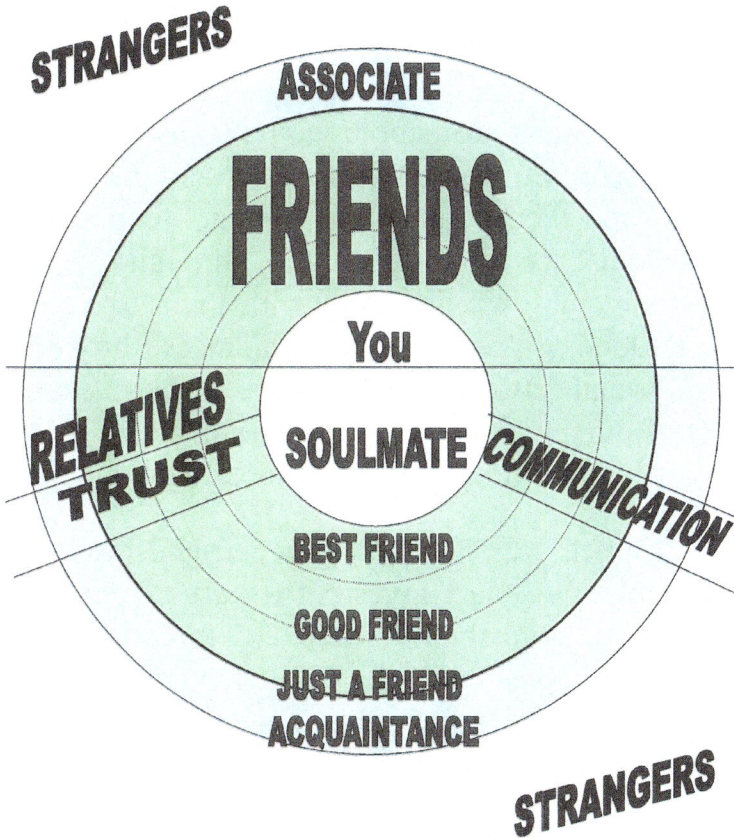

To have a better relationship with God, first I had to understand what relationships are. God called this illustration my Bull's-eye. Picture a dart board that has the bull's-eye in the middle with 4 rings around it. Each ring is a different level of a relationship. Outside the outer ring is void.

Working from the outside inward, we have strangers in the void, associates and acquaintances in the outer ring, the inner three rings are our levels of friendships, and the bull's-eye is our soul mate.

Strangers are people we have no interaction with. We see them everywhere and may even speak to them but there is no connection. Associates we meet generally through a work environment. We associate with them to get the work done. We meet acquaintances through a more social setting. We generally don't invest any part of ourselves in these relationships and are not involved or committed outside those settings.

When we start developing friendships, it is different. We start investing a part of ourselves into the relationship. There are three levels of friends: people that are just friends, our good friends, and our best friend. The levels depending on how much we invest of ourselves.

Our soul mate is the one person we have chosen to share our lives with, our spouse. Most of the time, our soul mate winds up being our total opposite. They are strong where we are weak, so we complement each other. We become one person! We consider our soul mate before ourselves. My husband is the half that makes me whole. I lean on his strength, enjoy his humor, and depend on his support.

"Relationships are built on trust,[5] through communication, to gain understanding, and sometimes requires compromise." This statement is direct, but let's break it down. To trust is to have belief in something or someone. When we have trust in someone, we have a confident hope! Trust is a charge we have custody of and must take care of. We must earn someone's trust and they must earn ours. If we are given their trust, we must protect it or we will lose it. The only way to build trust is by communication. We share information, thoughts, opinions, feelings, etc. We don't always agree but we gain understanding of that person. The more we build our level of trust, the more of ourselves we are willing to share. As we build trust, our relationships change from just friends to good friends, and if you're lucky, best friends. I have always been told, "If you have one best friend in a lifetime, you are very lucky." Through good or bad times, we know that we can truly depend on our good and best friends, and we value their opinion.

Becoming selfish and self-centered will destroy a relationship. If we are taking from but not giving of ourselves, the other person will stop being there for us since we're not there for them. If they are listening to us but we aren't listening to them, doesn't the other person feel hurt, rejected,

---

[5] Trust is the ability to rely on the integrity, strength, ability, and surety of a person.

and used? It could be us that are left feeling that way. A relationship without communication, understanding, or compromise is a one-sided relationship which can't and doesn't work.

There is also a friend that isn't included in our target and that is a bad friend. A bad friend tries to bring us down. They are the ones that want us to do things we know are wrong, but make it seem okay. When we are having trouble with someone or something, they feed into it. What I mean is, rather than helping us deal with the situation, they tell us things we want to hear to enhance and support the feelings we are already having: hurt, anger, bitterness, etc. These types of friends are not what we need in our life. They do not enhance who we are or help us grow.

Do you realize we are born with complete trust? As a newborn, we trust our parents to take care of us! We also learn to communicate from birth. We learn that if we cry a certain way, we get fed, get held or our diapers changed. Our parents learn to recognize our different cries. From birth, we are building a relationship with our parents. That trust can also be broken from birth.

As we grow, we also learn to compromise. If we are crying to be picked up and our parents just pat and rub our back, we are still receiving attention from them, and it will comfort us. This process occurs with everyone around us. We learn to recognize voices along with what type of response we can expect from each one. We are constantly defining and testing our boundaries. We can gain love, strength and support or suffer emotional and sometimes physical damage from those around us. Our family members will span all areas of our dartboard. They are in our lives whether we like them or not, and we tend to structure our other relationships based on them.

I grew up as an only child, so I didn't have the experiences that came with getting along with siblings. I have a lot of aunts, uncles, and cousins, but my father was in the military, so we didn't live around much family. Every other year, we spent two weeks with my father's family. Most of my best memories come from those vacations. It is hard to explain but even though I didn't spend much time with them, they range from acquaintances to best friends. I was around some more than others. Many have a special place in my heart because it was not the amount of time, but the quality of time spent. Our interests and outlooks will change as we get older and so may our friends, but our family is always there.

Most of the places we were based were close to some of my mother's family. We would sometimes meet with one of my uncles to go boating or dirt bike riding on weekends and I spent a lot of time at his house. He had two boys, so I was the little girl he never had, and I loved him for it. Yes, you could say he spoiled and doted on me a little. He and my aunt were like my good friends in the sense that they loved me unconditionally and protected me. They were always there for me, but the one relative I was closest to, was my maternal grandmother. She was always my safety net, my safe zone. I would spend four to six weeks with her every summer, and I always hated to go home. I can't express what she meant to me growing up. The day she went to be with our Lord, I knew three hours before I got the call. She never met a stranger, making friend where ever she went. She talked to everyone, and I never heard her say a bad word about anyone. Grandma had a God's heart. To this day, she has been the greatest influence in my life!

5. A RELATIONSHIP WITH GOD

Dartboard Illustration of Basic Relationships with God

STRANGERS

ASSOCIATE

FRIENDS

You

RELATIVES

TRUST

SOULMATE

GOD

COMMUNICATION

BEST FRIEND

GOOD FRIEND

JUST A FRIEND

ACQUAINTANCE

STRANGERS

Our relationship with God is very different from our human relationships, but in a lot of ways, the same. In a human relationship, we pick our friends to best support our interests and outlooks. In a relationship with God, we change through Him, our personalities, interests, and outlooks to best support God. It is more like having a relationship with a family member. He is there whether we want Him or not. He works behind the scenes sometimes and we don't even know or recognize it. He is our Father! He teaches us how to have other types of relationships and it is our choice to carry it over. Our relationship with Him will affect how we act or react to others and situations; what and how we say things; how we do things; how much we trust; and whether we fear or not. It is up to us as to what type of relationship we have with Him.

Through his grace, mercy, forgiveness, we are loved. His grace gives us what we don't deserve. His mercy doesn't give us what we do deserve, and His forgiveness is forever.

Until we are introduced to God, He is a stranger. He has no influence in our life. Once we have been introduced, we have a choice of whether He is an acquaintance or associate. As an acquaintance, we only know His name and a few facts about him. There is no involvement or interaction. As an associate, we only go to Him when we need something. We associate with Him to get the job done and then go on our merry way. Like an acquaintance, that is where our involvement or interaction stops.

When we develop feelings of affection and personal regard for Him and have the desire to learn more about Him, we will make Him a friend.

Our friendship with Him varies based on commitment or belief, connection, or interaction. These actions are developed through trust and communication. The more we communicate, the more we understand, and the more we trust in Him.

God is just a friend when we only communicate with Him in church. We may believe some of what the Bible says but not all. We enjoy His company when together but don't go out of our way to be with Him. In other words, we interact with Him when it is convenient for us.

He is our good friend when we go to church and read the Bible occasionally and pray once in a while. We share a lot of interests and enjoy being in His presence, but still do what we want to do. He speaks truth into our life, but we don't always take what He says to heart; we don't always listen.

God becomes our best friend when we pray daily, ask His advice and listen always. We read the Bible daily to seek His wisdom and understanding. A part of us is missing when we aren't together.

What I have learned is to have an intimate relationship with God; we must make Him our soul mate. As our soul mate, He is the principle of our life, feelings, thoughts, and actions. He is the spiritual part of us (We never leave home without

Him). He is the divine influence working in our hearts. He is the center, the innermost part of our total personality, THE CORE! He is our comrade, one of a pair; equal. An intimate relationship with Him is Him being the innermost, very personal, and private part of us resulting from close union. To have intimacy with Him is to have a detailed knowledge or deep understanding of what He wants for us. He is our coat or protection.

NIV John 3:30, *"He must become greater; I must become less."*

A relationship with God is the one relationship that starts off balance, just waiting to be developed and is there for everyone, but some people do not even know it. He has always had our best interest at heart and does not judge our past! He wants to be there for us all the time, not just when we need Him. From our birth, He wants to help us grow.

He comes offering help and many reject Him. He comes with understanding and support, but He is ignored. He comes with wisdom and advice, but they don't communicate with Him. He offers mercy and grace, but they are too proud to accept it. Others revere Him so highly that He is out of reach. They consider Him a part of their lives but can't communicate with Him. He is like a trophy on the wall. Sometimes it's because they don't know how and other times it's because they think they can't communicate. I am sorry to say these relationships are taking Him for granted. As I have mentioned before, a relationship without communication, understanding, and compromise can't and doesn't work.

This bears repeating, as I was growing up, I was not taught how to have a relationship with Him, only the laws to live by. I didn't know the goodness He had for me, only the punishment if I broke a law. I was taught the old covenant, not the new one. I didn't know I could talk to Him as a friend or advisor. I didn't know He would talk to me. I knew who He was, just like I knew who the guy living on the corner was, but I didn't know Him personally; He was not my friend! I knew He had a son that died for me, but I didn't understand what that really meant! Basically, I had information, but I didn't have understanding (revelation).

He is God! How many people do you know that have said, "What has God ever done for me?" My question to them is "What have you ever done for God?" As Americans, we are famous for "God Bless America", but I say "America, Bless God". See what I mean about one sided? The more we except from Him in our hearts, the more we give of ourselves. We let Him into our hearts the same as we do anyone else, by communicating, understanding, and compromising. Just because

He is the almighty God, we must remember He has feelings too.

To have a full relationship with God, we must understand the different aspects of the Holy Trinity: The Father, The Son, and Holy Spirit. They are equal, one is not greater than the other in their separate identities, and they are also one.

God (The Father) – He is the creator and operator. To put it simply, He is like the corporate head, the boss. He is responsible for the creation of the plan, mission, or job. Look to the Father because He is the giver of every good and perfect gift (The Source). In the Bible, when speaking of the Father, "of" is used: "the power of God", "the love of God", "the grace of God".

Jesus (The Son) – He is our Savior by giving his life for us. He represented God on earth. He is the administrator, responsible for the plan, mission, or job being carried out. Jesus is the giver of the source. In the Bible, Jesus is portrayed by "through", (give praise through the Son", "receive through the Son").

Holy Spirit (The Counselor) – He is our counselor, helper, intercessor, and friend. We can share our hopes, dreams, wants, and needs, basically we can share anything with Him. He carries messages between God, Jesus, and us. He helps us deal with things in a godly manner. He will never lead us astray. He is the power of the source. He is an active person and the one Jesus turned to during his time on earth. He is perfect, powerful, and glorious. In the Bible, Holy Spirit is portrayed by "in", ("walk in the spirit", "live in the Spirit"). Example: You ask the Father for healing in Christ's name. The Father gives the healing to Christ for it to be delivered to you. The Holy Spirit carries out the healing.

God is the best friend we can ever have if we let Him be. He wants to be our soul mate. Our relationship with Him is our choice. What type of relationship do you have with Him? What type do you want to have?

6. OUR BAGGAGE

When I came to God and accepted Jesus into my heart, I was carrying a lot of baggage with me. It was part of what caused me to hit rock bottom in the first place. We don't realize how much our past has in influencing our future. We act and react to today's facts and circumstances based on our past experiences. I'm not pointing fingers or laying blame on anyone in my past. My sole purpose is to build self-esteem and bring understanding. Sometimes it helps if we look at things from a different angle. God did that with me.

God showed me two illustrations to help sort out my baggage. I felt like I had so much, it was overwhelming and heavy. It was a task I couldn't do for myself because everything was so jumbled together. It's hard to climb our 'Ladder of Success' being so heavily weighed down. The first illustration is my backpack and the second is the fabric of who I am. They really go hand in hand. Everything we have put in our backpack (good or bad) has been woven into the fabric of who we are.

First, let's look at our backpack. He dealt with my baggage in two ways as I was climbing my ladder. At times, when He was teaching me something, He would have me pull a specific item out of my backpack. Generally, it had something to do with the way I reacted to a situation, but not always. When this happened, He would show me a different way (His way) to deal with it and His way would replace my way in my pack. Now everyone's baggage is going to be different. Eventually, He had me dump mine out and examine them. My baggage was represented by rocks that ranged from pea to bolder size. Next, we sorted my rocks out into three categories; 1. things done to me, 2. things I believed about myself, and 3. things I had done.

Did you know that things done to us are not our baggage to carry! I didn't. As long as I carried them, I was a victim. I've had people tell me rather flippantly but with good intent, "Let go, and Let God". They are sincere and only trying to help but if you don't know how, which I didn't, it doesn't help. In the situations of what was done to me, He showed me that 'let go and let God' meant to FORGIVE! When I truly forgave someone, I was no longer carrying that baggage. That doesn't mean it's erased from my past because it is woven into the fabric of who I am. (See how they work hand in hand). When I let go of it, the thread that was woven was removed. If you have ever run a colored piece of thread through a white piece of fabric; when it is removed, there is still residue left behind. We don't forget about it, but we stop letting it affect us anymore. The trick is, not to pick it back up. What I mean by not picking it back up is, stop talking or thinking about it. When we do that, we no longer look at ourselves as a victim but rather an overcomer. When I received this revelation, my load was probably cut in half.

When we are told things time and time again, especially when it comes from someone we look up to and respect, or our peers, we tend to believe them and start thinking of ourselves the same way. It's not good when these things are of a negative nature. Some of what God had me pull out of my backpack on my climb up my ladder fell in this area. He replaced them with what He said I am. 'I am loved, I am His chosen, I am worthy, I am capable, etc.' When I started looking at myself as God saw me, things around me changed. More threads removed from the fabric of who I am.

Lastly, the things we do. We as humans tend to carry our past forward into our future because they are the experiences we have to draw on. If we believe we deserved to be abused or what is said about us, eventually we will start abusing ourselves: drugs, alcohol, etc... Doesn't matter what it is, we don't deserve it from them or ourselves. Nor do we need to carry those experiences forward. Again, the biggest thing we can do is FORGIVE ourselves. God has! I have forgiven myself for the things I have done to myself, and I have strived to apologize to those around me that I have hurt. Most importantly, I try to use the tools God gave me to deal with situations now. I still stumble and fall but I keep getting up.

God's grace and mercy are already ours. Grace is receiving what we don't deserve, mercy is not receiving what we do deserve, and He has already forgiven us. He wants us to claim what is already ours and share it with others. We receive His faith, hope, and love.

Let God make changes in your life. Show love to the people around you. Show them there is hope. Be understanding, set the example and take them up with you instead of letting them bring you down. Notice I am not saying, "tell them". They will not receive what you say. I am saying be the example. Let them see the change in your life. Show them God's grace and mercy through those changes. Show God's love through what and how you say things. Be patient and understanding but most importantly, PRAY for them. We can only love God as much as the person we hate the most.

Prayer is our most important weapon. When we pray through Jesus' name, it will happen. Remember it is in God's time, not ours. Keep praying! When we pray for someone else, it brings change to us also. Here is an example:

Lord God, Heavenly Father, forgive (name) for what (he/she) (said/did). I forgive (him/her). Do whatever it takes to make a change in (him/her). If the change needs to be in me, show me what to do. Thank you for all the blessings you have bestowed on me and changing (whatever it is) in me! Amen!

To break the cycle, we must humble ourselves. If we do/say something out of line, apologize for it and let it go (Turn it over to God). Do not beat ourselves up about it. By apologizing, we are recognizing we did something wrong and are being honest about it. Apologizing is never easy and is very humbling, but the rewards are great. Like my pastor says, "Admit it, Quit it, and Forget it".

H - Handing
U - Up
M - My
I - Independence
L - Leaving
I - It
T - To
Y - Yahweh (God)

7. IT MAY BE YOU!

We are walking down the street and find a snake in our path, if we close our eyes so we can't see it, does it go away?

We are standing by our window and someone is yelling for help because they are being beaten up, if we plug our ears so we can't hear, are they out of danger?

We see a car accident with people still inside, if we cover our mouth and don't call for help, are they safe and unhurt?

Do these settings represent a part of the world we live in today? Instead of being a people believing in "One for all and all for one", we are only out for ourselves when it comes to day-to-day life. We have become indifferent to what is going on around us. We don't want to get involved. It's not our problem! If we ignore it, it will go away! It's just a part of life! I can't do anything about it anyway! Someone else will take care of it!

Why should it take a catastrophe for us to unite as one for the good of all and help our fellow man? Where are our hearts, compassion, and sense of justice?

It is amazing that the same people that close their eyes, ears and mouths are very vocal when it comes to what others should do, what should be done, how it should be done, and when it should be done. It is easy for someone to sit on the outside and look in but not get involved.

Have we ever used the phrase, "God helps those that help themselves" to justify doing something that seems selfish to others. Maybe we have beaten someone over the head with it when his/her problems have him/her so buried he/she can not breath. We may see someone with a problem, but decide it is not ours, so we are not concerned. To me, this phrase means I can't just sit around and wait for God to hand me what He wants for me. There has to be action on my part to deal with the imperfect world we all live in. Generally, my actions not only help me but also someone else at the same time. God does help people who help themselves by guiding them. Do you think He may use others to help get the job done? Everyone needs help at one time or another even if it is only encouragement. It may be a smile, kind word, guidance to get on their feet or a place to stay to be able to get there. I have always heard, "If you give a man a fish, you feed him for a day; if you teach a man to fish, you feed him for a lifetime".

We as humans are quick to judge others but not so quick to help them up when they fall. God does not want us to judge each other. He wants us to treat each other, as we would want to be treated. He wants us to turn to Him for help if we need it or don't know how to help someone else. He wants to know He can depend on us to do His good work.

It may be you that was put on the street to remove the snake to keep kids from being bitten.

It may be you that is meant to stop the person from being beaten to death by calling the police and being an eye witness at the trial. His arrest may be the turning point for the criminal to find God.

It may be you that is meant to call for an ambulance and save the life of the man in the car accident. His three-year-old daughter is probably looking out her window, waiting for her daddy to come home.

Most importantly, it may be you that is meant to be the godly example for the people that live around you. Someone that turns to God and away from his sins is the greatest witness for those around him. It may be you that makes the difference in someone's life through love, understanding, encouragement, a smile, or a hand. It may be you that is the one in need but by helping others, you also help yourself.

The facts and circumstances of how we got where we are don't matter, only where we are going when we accept Jesus as our Savior and confess our sins to him! God already knows what our sins are. He wants us to recognize and turn away from those sins with His help.

8. PREPERATIONS

In 2004, if someone would have told me what my next five years would be like, I would have run the other way. Can you say, BUT GOD! God started preparing me to walk through what was to come. I was about to have the opportunity to use all of what I learned and shared with you, plus more. When the question "Why do bad things happen to good people?" comes up, the biblical answer can be found in the book of Job in the Old Testament.

God gave me the book of Job to read, and I own it now. I didn't know it at the time, but it was in preparation for the future, and I still rely on it. He had a message for me, I just had to find it. I think I read it four or five times and each time, He would tell me, "No, you didn't get it, go read it again". I had picked up a few things in my reading but still wasn't getting the message He wanted.

Through my reading, God was giving me permission to sit in my pile of ashes and feel sorry for myself for a time, but not to stay there. He was also telling me it was ok to get mad at a situation. It was ok to yell, scream, and stomp my feet, not at the situation, but direct my anger to him about the situation. He gave me the opportunity to practice that one, and boy did I fail.

Ever gotten into an argument with someone that got so heated that one of you stormed off mad. I have! I have learned that it's not important who is right or wrong, but what is right or wrong. Someone close to me was going to do something I didn't think they should, and I was very direct with my opinion. They weren't listening to me. I lost my cool and told them to lose my phone number. I didn't want anything to do with them. I sat in my pile of ashes for about three days before my spirit was calm enough for me to hear God. When He did speak, I really didn't want to hear what he had to say. He explained to me that I wasn't upset because they weren't listening to me or taking my advice. I was upset because I was feeling rejected (Old Baggage). By rejecting my advice, they were rejecting me. He basically told me that my opinion didn't matter, but He went on to tell me why. Hard pill to swallow! He explained that it is ok to have an opinion and even voice it, but letting it affect me when they don't take the advice was my problem not theirs. He showed me that "our emotions are based on our opinion and rooted in judgment". I was standing in judgment of that person, not loving them. I had to go apologize. Now, I will tell someone what I think, but it's on them if they don't except it. Not my baggage to pick up!

The same can be said about expectations. When we (in our opinion) expect someone to do something and it doesn't happen, how do we let it affect us? The other person probably doesn't even know what's going on but we build anger and resentment towards them. We are judging that person based on our opinion.

I also learned that just because something bad happens doesn't mean I had a part in it or did something to make it happen. Job's friends kept telling him he must have done something to have caused his situation and wanted him to repent (perfect example of religious thinking). Remember God's grace and mercy! I didn't fully get the message God was trying to show me at the time, but if He can't get it to you one way, He will use another.

Something else God showed me was how to find my blessings. In my minds eye, I picture a blessing as being in a pristine box, wrapped in decorative paper, and finished off with a beautiful bow. That's not always the case! I had a situation presented to me that I was having a hard time wrapping my mind around.

God showed me that sometimes our biggest and best blessings are wrapped in comic paper with no bow, thrown in a mud puddle, and run over by a semi. Only by pealing off the muck and mire (facts and circumstances), can we find the blessing inside. In other words, it might not happen the way we think it should, but it doesn't make it any less of a blessing. My world was about to change!

9. WHEN THE WIND BLOWS

Part of the issue I was having "Before the Beginning" had to do with where I lived. I didn't want to be there and wanted to move. We had moved to the beach on the SW coast of Louisiana as a stopping off point when my husband retired from the Air Force, but we never left. Something God taught me was that I needed to be happy where I was. It doesn't matter what the facts and circumstances are, we should be happy in them. I had finally come to that resolution in my life. I adopted the attitude that I was double blessed. One day, I would have to leave my home and I would either have a home to go back to or I would get a new one. We had evacuated many times, and I always had a home to go back to. This time felt different. I can't tell this story without telling the whole story.

Let me set the stage! Hurricane Katrina had hit New Orleans a few weeks before, so my brother-in-law, his wife, and her mother had come to their camp on the beach and were planning on putting down roots since they lost their home. My elderly in-laws lived across the street. Our oldest daughter and my husband had essential jobs, and our youngest had just started college when Hurricane Rita came into the Gulf of Mexico. The news kept saying she was going to hit Galveston,

TX. Every inch of me was saying no, we are going to get it. My dad's family were calling for us to go to them, but Rita was projected to stall out where they live and I didn't want to be in her path.

The Wednesday before she made landfall, God told me to go empty our security box and take the contents with me. As many times as we had evacuated in the past, I had never done that. Our youngest came in with her boyfriend to help us pack out some things and drive my In-laws out. Her boyfriend convinced us to pack out the tools and he would take them to his house and store them for us. First time we did that also! (One of God's provisions) We took our off shore boat and my car inland to friends.

When we evacuated midday Thursday, Sept. 23rd, 2005, we knew it would be useless going north to the interstate, so we took the back way and caught the last run of the ferry east. I was leaving my husband and oldest daughter behind, but I couldn't dwell on the "what if's", only focus on what needed to be done. I was trusting God to protect them. I went with my in-laws to a friend, our youngest went to her boyfriend's parents, and my brother-in-law took his family to Baton Rouge to their sons. I might also say, our group had five vehicles, eight people, five dogs (one being a 90 lb German Shepard), two cats, and a gerbil.

My husband had asked me if I wanted to come home to an empty freezer or a stinky one. I chose the empty one. He and a friend were staying at our house that night, cooked up as much as they could and went around to feed all the stray cats in the neighborhood. How were we to know it was probably their last meal. The water had been turned off to the community, so they bathed in the neighbors above ground pool that night.

Friday was not a good day. My husband stayed in the parish until he just couldn't anymore to make sure everyone was out. I am watching the storm on TV as it is making its way to Galveston, NOT. The more I watched, the more I was convinced it was coming in on us and it did. I said goodbye to my house about 10 PM and calmly went to bed. The eye came ashore about 2 AM Saturday morning Sept. 25th and our community took a direct hit from the east wall of the storm. It was my mother-in-law's birthday, and she went to bed saying, "Happy Birthday to me!"

I had resigned myself that my home was gone but nothing could have prepared me for the aerial photos we saw Sunday. The whole community was wiped off the face of the map. There was nothing! I broke down crying and at the same time, the house phone was ringing. It was my family wanting me to come. I told them I would as soon as I was able, got myself together, and started making plans. The people we were staying with needed to help their family that had been impacted. I needed to make arrangement for my in-laws to be driven to Houston because they were refusing to go with me. I didn't feel I could go with them because of our animals. I had to call someone who I had only meet once to take them up on the offer to stay with them until I could get all my ducks in a row which took about a week.

Our oldest was having to live at her job because her mobile home was damaged and off its blocks. My husband was living in a motel that had been opened to them to ride the storm out. With the animals, I couldn't stay with him. Our youngest couldn't go back to school due to damage the college sustained. We had been able to go get her truck at least.

The parish was kept closed until the following Friday to make it safe. As soon as it opened, our youngest went down. From the air, it looked like everything was gone but, on the ground, she could walk a debris path and identify things from our house. Anything wood had been washed away. She called me to say she had found one of my grandmother's plates. I didn't believe her because I thought I had packed all of them out a few years before and put them in storage. Each one had a saying on it, so I told her to read it to me. Guess I was wrong! When God wants you to get a message and you don't get it the first time, He will find a way. I didn't get it with Job, but I got it this time. It was the story of the sparrow and the robin.

"Robin - Why are these human
beings running around
anxious so?

Sparrow - Because they don't
have a heavenly Father like
you and me!"

When she read that, it was like a ton of bricks hit me. God was trying to tell me he was in control and to trust His lead. I literally threw my hands up and told him I trusted Him and wasn't going to stress or be anxious over anything. Through everything that followed, I could tell by the peace I felt that God had this. The most amazing thing was the porcelain plate would have been hanging in my kitchen. The whole house was gone, but the plate was still on our property. It didn't have a nick or chip in it and still had the original plastic string on the back to hang it up. I was able to go down a few days later and found a few more things that were salvageable.

You might be asking how I could look at the lose of my home as a blessing, it is all in perspective. 1. By the whole house being gone, I didn't have anything to repair or clean up, just replace with an upgrade. 2. My in-laws were getting to the age that the family was going to have to have the hard conversation about them living alone. God moved them for us!

By now it is Monday and I had all my ducks taken care of. Our youngest and I left heading north. My plan was to stay in one of my cousins back rooms or her travel trailer. When we got there, a temporary fence had been put up so I would have a place for our three dogs to go outside. Yes, one of them was the Shepard. God already had plans for me laid out. On Tuesday we went to the FEMA office that had been set up in the area. We were the last walk-ins they took that day. Everyone else had to make appointments. We had taken photos and had them developed before we left and the FEMA reps were shocked to see the devastation. They assured us we would have our emergency assistance by Thursday.

Next was to file for emergency food stamps. Thinking back, it was a test of my faith in God. Come to find out, the state we were in didn't recognize Rita as a national disaster, so I had to fill out a full application. I did, even though I knew I wouldn't qualify under normal circumstances. Yes, I was denied. Accepting the denial, we went back to my cousins.

That night, one of my other cousins came over. She asked if her sister had talked to me yet. I had no clue what she was talking about. Long story short, the people that had been renting my aunt's house had skipped the day I got there (Another of Gods provisions). They offered it to me rent free for as long as I needed. It was a two bedroom, fully furnished, fully equipped, handicap accessible home. My in-laws would have been very comfortable if they had come. I explained I would only except the house if I could pay the house payment and utilities. It was still a blessing because of the cost difference to our previous home on the beach. Accepting a blessing when it is at the expense of another to me is taking advantage, and I couldn't do that when finances weren't the problem. We moved in the next day, and I was there for the next three months. We moved the temporary fence for the dogs, so they didn't have to be on a leash all the time.

I spoke with our oldest the next week and the subject of emergency food stamps came back up. She insisted I go back and try again, so I did. What did I have to lose? Again, I was denied but this time the lady I was dealing with caught me before I left and suggested I go across the state line to an effected state and try there. It was only 30 miles, so away we went. It didn't take long to file and when we got ready to leave, the lady suggested I not tell anyone in the waiting room what I qualified for (Another Gods Provision). There were people there from that state that didn't qualify for anything because their zip code wasn't listed as an effected area. We qualified for three months instead of one due to our zip code being listed not only for Rita, but for Katrina also.

After the first week, our youngest went back to stay with her boyfriend's parents, and was finally able to get her stuff from the dorms at the college. She got a job, and enrolled in college where she was. I would make trips down to visit every few weeks. A friend had lent my husband a travel trailer to stay in, so we were settling into a new norm. The only thing left was to get our oldest settled. She was still sleeping at work or on friends' couches.

After about a month, the insurance finally settled on her mobile home, so she had the money to do something else. There had been two ladies living across the street from her. They had evacuated with their neighbor, but on the way back, they got separated. When they did arrive, there was only one of them. Her story was they had gotten a phone call that there was a family emergency so the other one had flown back west. She offered to sell our daughter their mobile home, saying that hurricanes weren't their thing. She had come back to take care of things and then go join the other lady. I had gone down to help make sure the paperwork and deal was on the up and up because she was selling cheap and leaving some contents in the process. Everything seemed to be ok even though we had a feeling it was to good too be true. We needed to do something to provide her a place to live. Not every blessing is from God. We should have listened.

We are blessed to be a blessing. The local church I was attending had a guest speaker come. He was with a Christian organization that helped in catastrophes. The pastor gave him my contact information but with not having a home, I couldn't use his help. I had meet a lady that could use the help before I left to go north. Her insurance company had cancelled her the year before because of the age of her home. Rita had lifted the roof so it was raining down her interior walls. To make matters worse, she was in the wrong zip code to qualify for FEMA. She missed it by one street. I gave him her contact information and within two weeks, the repairs were done, and she had a new roof. God doesn't need our help, He only needs our cooperation.

God had given me a promise that I would be home by the first of the year and I was holding on to that. In November, my husband took some time off and came up just before Thanksgiving. The parish had a meeting the day before he was to go back. When he got the call telling him what had come out of the meeting, to say I lost it is an understatement. My peace was out the window, and I was doing some ranting and raving in the background because of what it meant for us to be able to go back to the beach. The information was contrary to the promise God had given me. The next day, he left, and I was on the phone to my home church for guidance. I was given some scriptures to read and pray over. My next call was to my cousin to get permission to go to the local church to throw myself on the alter and just be in His presence. With that granted, my bible, CD player, and praise and worship music in tow, off I went. It took me three hours to start calming down. It took another couple of days for my spirit to get quiet enough to hear God. (I was sitting in my pile of ashes.) When He did speak, it was like a light bulb coming on and my peace was back. "I promised you'd be home for the first of the year, but I didn't say where home would be." I called my husband and shared this with him.

My next trip down was in mid December and we started looking for alternatives further inland. We made the decision to keep the probability that his parents would be living with us in our decision making process. I knew God had a place for us, we just had to find it. We were able to find a piece of property that was already ready for a mobile home or a house to be built and it was at a reasonable price. As a matter of fact, it wasn't even for sale but the owner was willing to part with it.

We had been on the list for a FEMA trailer, but they wouldn't place one in a flood zone (where we had needed it). After we purchased the property, we changed the requested location. We were told it should only take a few days. I headed back up north to pack up and wait for the call that said we had the trailer. Between what I had taken up with me and what I had been buying to replace items, I was going to have a truck load. I had to make wood slates for the side of the truck. I bought a blue tarp incase it rained, and a yellow rope to tie it all down with. I was ready and waiting, and waiting, and waiting. Finally on January 15, 2006 we made the decision for me to make the move whether the trailer was there or not. I had the cats in their crates in each corner of the extended cab on top of stuff. Two of the dogs in the middle of them, in a dog bed. The German Shepard had the whole passenger seat, and the bed of the truck was loaded, covered, and strapped down. The gerbil found a new home with a friend's daughter. To say I was loaded to the gills would be an accurate description. So, on January 17th, I made the trip home. My husband was at the property doing some work and as I pulled onto the property, he got a phone call. The dogs hadn't even been unloaded yet and the FEMA trailer pulled onto the property. Can you say, 'stepping out in faith'. It took two days for the trailer to be set up and we moved in. I was home for the first of the year!

Meanwhile, we only knew the nicknames of the ladies our oldest daughter got the mobile home from. We didn't have any reason to question anything when we did the paperwork with the notary. About this time, we found out the one that sold her the mobile home wasn't the one that owned it. She had murdered the owner and stolen her identity. She also stayed with our daughter for a week after the sale. But God! We only found this out because she turned herself in saying she was afraid she would do it again. Our daughter had to relinquish the mobile home and everything else to the rightful owner's family and was out the money. We did find her a nice house to buy at that point. Sometimes, we settle for what is easy rather than waiting for God's best.

My in-laws had a friend go to Houston and move them to a small town about 45 minutes to the east of us. She moved in with them to help as their care giver and driver. This made us feel better, having them closer, and with someone there to help them.

I have learned that if I let God lead, He will not only show up, but He will also show off. Like the property, I knew God had a house for us, we just had to find it. Knowing what we wanted and the amount of money we had to spend, we started shopping for mobile homes. I wanted a sliding glass door in the dining room, I didn't want to have to go through the bathroom to get to the closet, and I didn't want to walk on carpet coming from outside to a bathroom. Over the next month or so we looked locally and in Texas, but nothing fit the bill. We decided we would go east and work our way back because someone we knew had found a nice one in Opelousas. Our intention was to start where they had gotten theirs, but we over shot it and couldn't turn around until we came to another lot so that was our starting point. But God! The salesman showed us the size we thought was in our price range, but nothing jumped out at us. We were getting ready to leave and he said he had another one that was bigger than what we were looking for and was in our price range. We learned never to put limits on God. When we walked into that mobile home's living room, I was staring at a sliding glass door in the dining room. I went right and my husband went left. As I went into the kitchen, there was another doorway into the utility room. Guess what, there was a back door in the utility room and another doorway leading to the master bath with another door into the master bedroom (No carpet in-between)! The closet separated the master bedroom from the living room and there was yet another door that led back to the living room. It had everything we were looking for and more. All I could do was yell down the hall to my husband that it was "SOLD". His response was 'but you haven't seen this end yet. I didn't need to; it was what we were looking for. We had been looking at ones with three bedrooms and this was four, plus it had a second living area with a built-in TV and theater system. Perfect for a two-family household. We did have to measure the place where we were going to have it put and have the movers come to make sure they could get it on the property. But God! It would fit and the movers could do it. In April, I was standing at the head of our driveway crying "I have a home" as it was being brought in and put on our property. By May, we were moving the in-laws in with us.

Since then, God was there when our youngest was in a car accident that almost totaled my car, and our oldest being involved in two wrecks that totaled her cars. He walked me through everything it took to care for my in-laws until they graduated to be with our Lord in 2008 and 2009, and the passing of my father in 2017. Our new home has been through three hurricanes since Hurricane Rita; Hurricane Ike (Cat. 4), Laura (Cat. 5), and Delta (Cat 3) with minimum to no damage. The list of God's faithfulness has gone on and on and on. We have been blessed beyond the loss of our house.

Through everything, I can always tell when I have my focus on the facts and circumstances rather than my faith in God. My peace and joy is gone. Anxiety and stress will take it's place.

10. TRANSFORMATION

God has probably put people and situations in place to help you, but you must choose God for yourself. If you are ready to make that choice:

> *(NLT) Romans 10:9-11, For if you confess with your mouth that Jesus is Lord and believe in your heart God raised him from the dead, you will be saved. For it is by believing in your heart that you are made right with God, and it is by confessing with your mouth that you are saved. As the scriptures tell us, "Anyone who believes in him will not be disappointed."*

When you start going to church, there may be things going on that you don't understand. You may be feeling leery of or even inhibited by things you see and hear. Perhaps you are afraid to ask questions because you don't want to appear stupid. Don't be afraid to ask anything. God, Jesus, and Holy Spirit are great subjects for Christians to share. Find a mature believer and let him/her guide you.

You know you belong with God in your life. You know you want what other people have, but you question what is it and how do you get it? It is a feeling of total peace and happiness that radiates from them. It is becoming one with God! This is the best way I can explain it. It is like standing naked in a warm and brilliant light, being bathed in the love of Jesus. It is a blanket of strength, security, and protection. I don't mean naked as in "no clothes". I mean, open yourself up to Him. Be an open book and don't try to hide things. It is turning yourself over to the Lord to accept any changes he may deem necessary. Change comes by dealing with our baggage. Don't worry about what you don't have yet because you do have it! God has given us everything we need; it is just a matter of understanding where and how to find it in ourselves. Here is some knowledge to help in understanding what I have said.

Every one of us is different because we have experienced different situations, whether by birth, circumstance, or by choice. When we declare Jesus as our Savior, our sins are forgiven. They are gone, but those same sins have left a residue in the fabric of who we are. This is what we call baggage. We all have baggage of some type or another, and no one is exempt. Baggage from circumstances is not necessarily the circumstance itself, but the feelings that those circumstances have left us with. The feelings may be hate, bitterness, unforgiveness, resentment etc… that we carry. Most of life's hurts are carried in our emotions. Things such as how we react to others, what we say, how we say it, what we fear, and how we do things have been determined by our environment.

Scripture speaks of acquiring a new heart. Is our heart just a muscle that keeps blood circulating in our bodies, or is it more? Have you ever heard the phrase? "The heart is the window to the soul!" Don't we describe it as the center of our personality? We relate our feelings and emotions to our hearts. Let's look at some examples:

"Have a heart" - We ask someone to be compassionate or merciful. We also describe someone who is compassionate or merciful as having a heart.

"Have one's heart in the right place" – We use this phrase to describe someone that is fundamentally kind or generous.

"From the bottom of our heart" – We use these words to express complete sincerity.

"Hardhearted" – This is said to describe someone that is mean, uncompromising, crass, rude, and unfeeling towards others.

"Change of heart" – This means someone has had a change in his or her opinion or view on something.

Get my point? There are many phrases involving the heart. If our personality is in our heart, then to change the fabric of who we are, we must have a change of heart. What God wants for us is to have a change of heart so we can have our hearts in the right place to walk in the full glory He has already given us.

Humility is another important key to remember, and humbling oneself is not something you can plan for or anticipate, nor is it something we can do on our own. It is by God, and in His time, not ours. God is continually taking us to new levels, showing us new things. Remember from earlier?

H - Handing
U - Up
M - My
I - Independence
L - Leaving
I - It
T - To
Y - Yahweh (God)

The best description of being humble is to destroy the independence, power, or will of oneself.

To have humility is to have a courteous respect for something and a modest sense of one's own importance. If you have ever said "I was wrong!" then you have humbled yourself. We need to stay open to change. God will show us what needs changed, and it may be something we thought was not a problem, or something we thought we had dealt with, buried away in the past. He wants to teach us how to deal with our past in a godly manner and make true peace with it so as not to let it be a part of our Christian walk in the present and future.

Integrity is another word that should describe a Christian. God wants to build integrity in us. God wants us to have ethical principles, a moral character, and maturity. Don't think this will happen overnight. Maturity is a slow process, a lifelong pursuit. Again, it is in God's time not ours. Waiting on Him sometimes isn't easy, but worth it. He uses our baggage to humble our hearts and to build integrity. We are growing in who we are through him.

W - Why
A - Am
I - I
T - Talking

The Bible gives us knowledge. Knowledge is to know things in our mind. How many people do you know that are book smart but don't have common sense? Our ability to humble ourselves gives us understanding. Understanding is to be able to apply what we know, and wisdom knows when to apply it. We can gain knowledge, but God gives us understanding and wisdom if we let Him in our hearts.

If you have read this whole book and are saying to yourself, "I know all that", you probably do. Ask yourself if you are applying it to your everyday life. If not, you have the knowledge but not the understanding or wisdom. What I want for you is what God wants for you, and that is to come to know what HE has already given you. I want you to gain the full understanding of His ways and possess the wisdom in His Word. As H. W. Van Loon was quoted as saying in Webster's Dictionary, "rise a few rungs on the social scale". My social scale is my spiritual ladder of success. God is the object of my climb, and He is my destiny.

11. FINAL NOTE

When you picked up this book, you made a choice; you wanted success. When you continued reading after the warning; you wanted a change to take place in your life. Each time you finished a chapter and continued reading, you wanted to know more. You are hungry for what He has for you. There is much more to learn, it is found in the Bible and through fellowship with God. God will not disappoint you!

Start by finding a quiet place and just talking to God as you would your closest friend. Open your mind and heart to receive what He has to say to you. Take what he says to heart no matter whether you like it or not. If you don't like what he says, it is probably something you need to change with his help. He will never put more on us than we can handle. Strive to stay in God's presence by listening to Christian radio and reading His word. Find a church to celebrate and thank God for what He is doing in you.

When you accepted Him in your life, the person you were is gone. You are a new person in Christ. Integrity is a firm adherence to a code of morals or artistic values. Your integrity will come from Him. Each day you are in his presence, strive to learn more, and apply what you learn; you are growing, and your integrity is increasing. If you make a mistake, apologize for it, and forget it. Don't beat yourself up over it. Reject any form of doubt or condemnation that comes from the world around you that may lead to your rejecting God. When you stop seeking His presence, your growth will stop. Stay hungry for Him and loving toward others! It is not hard with God's help; just ask Him when in doubt.

The facts and circumstances around you are still going to be there. God is going to teach you how to walk through them in a different way. I would like for you to write these two statements down and put them somewhere you will see every day. The first is "God LOVES me!" He loves all of us and knows we are not perfect. The Second is "The problem isn't the problem. The problem is my ATTITUDE about the problem." God will give the understanding of what this statement means and how to apply it to everyday life as you walk with Him. Talk to God and ask the Holy Spirit for help to deal with every situation that may face you through out each day.

Personalize scriptures as you read the Bible. Here is an example:

> NIV Isaiah 30:18-21, *"Yet the Lord longs to be gracious to (name); He rises to show (name) compassion. For the Lord is a God of justice. Blessed is (name) who wait(s) for*

Him. (Name) will weep no more. How gracious He will be when (name) cries for help! As soon as He hears, He will answer (name). Although the Lord gives (name) the bread of adversity and the water of affliction, (name) teachers will be hidden no more; with (name) own eyes (name) will see them. Whether (name) turn to the right or the left, (name) ears will hear a voice' behind (name), saying, "This is the way; walk in it.""

You are a Blessing and a child of God! Believe!

NOTES

Printed in Great Britain
by Amazon